If I Could Write This in Fire

If I Could Write This in Fire

MICHELLE CLIFF

 University of Minnesota Press

Minneapolis

London

Material in this book appeared previously or in earlier forms in *The American Voice* (Winter 1992); *IKON* (1986); *Hotel Amerika* (2004); *eleveneleven* (2005); and *Michigan Quarterly Review* (Spring 2006).

Excerpt from *Jamaica,* by Andrew Salkey, is reprinted with kind permission from Patricia Salkey.

Translations of poetry by Federico García Lorca and Pier Paolo Pasolini by Michelle Cliff.

Every effort has been made to obtain permission to reproduce previously published material in this book. If any proper acknowledgment has not been made, we encourage copyright holders to contact the publisher.

Published by THE UNIVERSITY OF MINNESOTA PRESS
111 Third Avenue South, Suite 290
Minneapolis, MN 55401-2520
http://www.upress.umn.edu

LIBRARY OF CONGRESS CATALOGING-IN-PUBLICATION DATA
Cliff, Michelle.
    If I could write this in fire / Michelle Cliff.
        p.   cm.
    ISBN 978-0-8166-5474-1 (acid-free paper)   ISBN 978-0-8166-5475-8 (pbk.: acid-free paper)
    1. Cliff, Michelle. 2. Authors, Jamaican—20th century—Biography. 3. Authors, American—20th century—Biography. 4. Jamaican Americans—Biography. 5. Lesbian authors—Biography. I. Title.
    PR9265.9.C55Z46 2008
    813'.6—dc22   2008021743

Printed in the United States of America on acid-free paper

The University of Minnesota is an equal-opportunity educator and employer.

15 14 13 12 11 10 09 08   10 9 8 7 6 5 4 3 2 1

Contents

Journey into Speech

All o' we losin' out,
'cause we won't own up to weself,
grab we soul,
grab weself like we know weself,
an' tradition up we tradition,
an' fuck the nex' man
who laugh after we
an' say it small
an' slave-make
an' fragment-up
an' dark night as Dung'll
—Andrew Salkey, *Jamaica*

To route this journey I must begin with origins, and the significance of these origins. How they have made me the writer that I am.

I begin in the Caribbean, specifically on the island of Jamaica, and although I have lived in the United States and in England, I travel this world as a Jamaican. Jamaica forms my writing for the most part, and for the most part has formed me.

Put simply, Jamaica is a place halfway between Africa and England, although historically one culture has been esteemed and the other denigrated (both of these are understatements)—at least among the Afro-Saxons of my childhood. As a child among these people, indeed of these people, I received the message of anglocentrism, of white supremacy, and I internalized it. Even as I suspected its wrongness. As a writer, as a human being, I have had to search for what was lost to me from the darker side, and for what has been hidden, to be dredged from memory and dream. As my writing delved longer and deeper into this part of myself, I began to dream and to imagine. I became able to envision Nanny, the leader of a group of guerrilla fighters known as the Windward Maroons, as she is described: an old Black woman naked except for a necklace made from the teeth of white men. I began to love her.

One of the effects of indoctrination, of passing into the anglocentrism of British West Indian culture, is that you believe absolutely in the hegemony of the King's English and in the proper forms of expression. Or else your writing is not literature; it is folklore, or worse. And folklore can never be art. Read some poetry by West Indian writers—some, not all—and you will see what I mean. The reader has to dissect anglican stanza after anglican stanza for Caribbean truth, and may never find it. The anglican ideal—Milton, Wordsworth, Keats—was held before us with an assurance that we were unable, and would never be able, to achieve such excellence. We crouched outside the cave.

To write as a complete Caribbean writer demands of us retracing the African part of ourselves, reclaiming as our own and as our subject a history sunk under the sea, or scattered as potash in the canefields, or gone to bush, or trapped within a class system notable for its rigidity and for its dependence on color stratification.

On a past bleached from our minds. It means re-creating the art forms of our ancestors and speaking in the *patois* forbidden us. It means realizing our knowledge will always be wanting. It means also, I think, mixing in the forms taught us, undermining the oppressor's language and co-opting, or corrupting, his style, and turning it to our purpose. In my novel *No Telephone to Heaven*, I alternate the King's English with *patois,* not only to indicate the class background of characters but to show how Jamaicans operate within a split consciousness. It would be as dishonest for me to write the novel entirely in *patois* as it would be to write it entirely in the King's English. Nor is *No Telephone to Heaven* a linear construction; its subject is the political upheavals of the 1970s and 1980s. Therefore I mix time and incident and place and character and also form to try to mirror the chaos of the times.

We are a fragmented people. My experience as a writer coming from a culture of colonialism, a culture of Black people riven from one another, my struggle to achieve wholeness from fragmentation, while working within fragmentation, producing work which may find its strength in its depiction of fragmentation, through form as well as content, is similar to other writers whose origins are in countries defined by colonialism.

Ama Ata Aidoo, the Ghanaian writer, in *Our Sister Killjoy, or Reflections from a Black-Eyed Squint* (Lagos and New York: NOK Publishers, 1979), plots this fragmentation, showing how both the demand and the solace of the so-called mother country can claim us while we long for our homeland and are shamed for it and ourselves at the same time. The form Aidoo uses to depict this dilemma of colonial peoples—part prose, narrative and epistolary, part poetry — reflects the fragmented state of the protagonist and grasps her fury, living in Europe but drawn back to Ghana, knowing she can never be European. She will only be a "been-to" — that is, one who has been to the mother country. *Our Sister Killjoy* affected me directly, not just because like Aidoo's heroine I was a been-to. I was drawn by the way Aidoo expresses rage against colonialism — crystallized for her by the white man she calls the "Christian Doctor" throughout, he who excises Black African hearts to salvage white South African lives. In her pellucid rage Aidoo's prose breaks apart into a staccato poetry — direct, short, brilliantly bitter — as if measured prose would disintegrate under her fury.

I wanted that kind of clarity in my writing as I came closer into contact with my rage and a realization that rage could fuel and shape my work. As a light-skinned colonial girlchild, both in Jamaica and in the Jamaican milieu of my family abroad, rage was the last thing expected of me.

After reading Aidoo I knew I wanted to tell exactly how things were, what had been done, to us and by us, without muddying (or whitening) the issue with conventional beauty, avoiding becoming trapped in the seductive grace of language for its own sake.

After I read *Our Sister Killjoy* something was freed in me; I directed rage outward into creativity rather than inward. In a piece entitled "If I Could Write This in Fire, I Would Write This in Fire," I was able to let myself go; any thought of approval for my words vanished. I strung together myth, dream, historical detail, observation, as I had done before, but I added native language, tore into the indoctrination of the colonizer, and surprised myself with the violence of my words. That piece of writing led to other pieces in which I tried to depict personal fragmentation and describe political reality, according to the peculiar lens of the colonized—but one aware of itself. These essays are a result of that informed gaze.

And What Would It Be Like

I

And what would it be like
The terrain of my girlhood

[with you]   There is no map

Ok.
Mangoes
then the sweet liquidity of star apple
custard apple
sweetsop
cut with sharp tamarind
washed down with coconut water
ginep   slippery
papaya
where restless baby-ghosts vent their furies

all devoured
against trade winds
                    Will I eternally return to the Trade?

Then—
there's more
by which I mean
hibiscus, jasmine, night-blooming   and otherwise
by which I mean
the more ancient
pre-Columbian   pre-Contact
growth
Edenic underbrush
unyielding   thick as a woman's thatch
like the [girls' school legend] un-drawered tennis mistress
who
or whom
we slid beneath
to glimpse the bright, thick ginger
womanly—
God, we wanted to be women, never knowing what that meant.
—patch
thatch so thick you'd never guess she was British
[our prejudice]

And banana leaves
wide as a girl's waist—sometimes
and as long as a girl's feathered legs
which exude the juice of the fruit
without a taste of the fruit
dependable as any aunt

down a falls once owned by an aunt
we flowed
on the impossible green
into the equally impossible blue
lit by the height of an impossible light
taking our half-naked selves
down the sweet
into the salt
water
and women
women
and water
my grandmother's river
my distant aunt's falls
no one else was allowed in
other children   [that didn't feel right]
revolutionaries are made, not born.

II

Bougainvillea
grows
[according to the botanist]
in showy profusion—
but scentless—
disappoints

III

Under the high-leggéd mahogany bed
caciques at each corner   like apostles
or caryatids
the tail of a scorpion is set to strike
transparent   dangerous
I know its poison.

IV

All feels wild from this distance.

V

One time at Cable Hut
I fell into a sinkhole
down and down and down
but came back up
suddenly
One time I had my period and swam way out
past the coral reef
and wondered if a shark would be drawn to me
as the warm salt drew the blood out   and the sea roared
One time I speared a lobster clean   underwater at Lime Key
One time I brushed beside the flimsy nightdress
of a jellyfish   and have a mark on my thigh to prove it
One time I dodged an alligator in a swamp by the Carib's edge

my mouth gorged on a hundred oysters   their grit becoming
pearl against my teeth
One time I played with a cousin's cock underwater—
he taught me to shoot coconuts between the eyes so they
rained around us on the sand   it was the least I could do
Those were the dangerous days
There was nothing to stop us   it seemed

VI

There is no map
only the most raggéd path back   to
my love   so much so
she ended up in the bush
                        at a school where such things were
taken very seriously   severely
                and
I was left   missing her   never ceasing
                and
she was watched   for signs
                and
I was left   alone   missing her   never ceasing
                and
she was not allowed to write   at least she never did
                and
I walked the length and breadth of the playing fields
                                I have never felt so lost
not like that

                        and
I wanted to be dead   that's all
                                        finally
the headmistress and head girl found me
in the stacks
                    weeping
                                    violently
against spines of biology
                        running into history
I can see myself in the lapsed documentary of memory
                            curled up against books, shelves
salting the sea island cotton of my blouse
                        wanted to lose my
self   water tearing down my face, school badge
with cross & crown   & Latin motto
                    my parents were summoned
the word was not spoken
                            I was told to forget everything
I would never see her again   I would never see her again
            except with my mind's eye   and to this day
golden
                    they rifled my hiding place
ransacked my words   read me aloud   on the
verandah
                    under the impossible sun
my father   uttering
"When you're twenty we'll laugh about this."
                    that I remember

they took me, on the advice of the doctor who delivered
me,
                        to Doctor's Cave
which is a beach, not Prospero's vault,
                    for weeks
I swam
            like Caliban
her feathered legs opening under water   salt rushing into me
                    I was exhausted, they said
excitable

I wanted to be a wild colonial girl
And for a time, I was.

If I Could Write This in Fire,
I Would Write This in Fire

I

We were standing under the waterfall at the top of Orange River. Our chests were just beginning to mound—slight hills on either side. In the center of each were our nipples, which were losing their sideways look and rounding into perceptible buttons of dark flesh. Too fast it seemed. We touched each other, then, quickly and almost simultaneously, raised our arms to examine the hairs growing underneath. Another sign. Mine were wispy and light-brown. My friend Zoe had dark hair curled up tight. In each little patch the riverwater caught the sun, so we glistened.

The waterfall had come about when my uncles dammed the river to bring power to the sugar mill. Usually when I say "sugar mill" to anyone not familiar with the Jamaican countryside or for that matter my family, I can tell their minds cast an image of tall smokestacks, enormous copper cauldrons, a man in a broad-brimmed hat with a whip, several dozens of slaves—that is, if they have any idea of how large sugar mills once operated. It's a grandiose expression, like plantation, verandah, out-building.

(Try substituting farm, porch, outside toilet.) To some people it even sounds romantic.

Our sugar mill was little more than a round-roofed shed, which contained a wheel and a woodfire. We paid an old man to run it, tend the fire, and then either bartered or gave the sugar away, after my grandmother (my mother's mother) had taken what she needed. Our canefield was about two acres of flat land next to the river. My grandmother had six acres in all—one donkey, a mule, two cows, some chickens, a few pigs, and stray dogs and cats who had taken up residence in the yard.

Her house had four rooms, no electricity, no running water. The kitchen was a shed in the back with a small pot-bellied stove. Across from the stove was a mahogany counter, which had a white enamel basin set into it. The only light source was a window, a small space covered partly by a wooden shutter. We washed our faces and hands in enamel bowls with cold water carried in kerosene tins from the river and poured from enamel pitchers. Our chamber pots were enamel also, and in the morning we carefully placed them on the steps at the side of the house where my grandmother collected them and disposed of their contents. The outhouse was about thirty yards from the backdoor—a "closet" as we called it—infested with lizards capable of changing color. When the door was shut, it was totally dark, and the lizards made their presence known by the noise of their scurrying through the torn newspaper, or the soft shudder when they dropped from the walls. I remember most clearly the stench of the toilet, which seemed to hang in the air in that climate.

But because every little piece of reality exists in relation to another piece, our situation was not that simple. It was to our yard that people came with news first. It was in my grandmother's parlor that the Disciples of Christ held their meetings.

Zoe lived with her mother and sister on borrowed ground in a place called Breezy Hill. She and I saw each other almost every day on our school vacations over a period of three years. Each morning early — as I sat on the cement porch with my coffee cut with condensed milk — she appeared: in her straw hat, school tunic faded from blue to gray, white blouse, sneakers hanging around her neck. We had coffee together, and a piece of hard-dough bread with butter and cheese, waited a bit and headed for the river. At first we were shy with each other. We did not start from the same place.

There was land. My grandparents' farm. And there was color.

(My family was called *red*. A term which signified a degree of whiteness. "We's just a flock of red people," a cousin of mine once said.) In the hierarchy of shades I was considered among the lightest. The countrywomen who visited with my grandmother commented on my "tall" hair — meaning long. Wavy, not curly.

I had spent the years from three to ten in New York and spoke — at first — like an American. I wore American clothes: shorts, jeans, bathing suit. Because of my American past I was looked upon as the creator of games. Cowboys and Indians. Cops and Robbers. Peter Pan.

(While the primary colonial identification of Jamaicans was English, American colonialism was a strong force in my childhood—and of course continues today. We were sent American movies and American music. American aluminum companies had already discovered bauxite on the island and were shipping the ore to their mainland. United Fruit bought our bananas. White Americans came to Montego Bay, Ocho Rios, and Discovery Bay for their vacations, and their cruise ships docked in Kingston and Port Antonio and other places. In some ways America was seen as a better place than England by many Jamaicans. The farm laborers sent to work in American agribusiness came home with dollars and gifts and new clothes; there were few who mentioned American racism. Many of the middle class who emigrated to Brooklyn or Staten Island or Manhattan were able to pass into the white American world—saving their blackness for other Jamaicans or for trips home; in some cases, forgetting it altogether. Those middle-class Jamaicans who could not pass for white managed differently—not unlike the Bajans in Paule Marshall's *Brown Girl, Brownstones*—saving, working, investing, buying property. Completely separate in most cases from Black Americans.)

I was someone who had experience with the place that sent us triple features of B-grade westerns and gangster movies. And I had tall hair and light skin. And I was the granddaughter of this grandmother. So I had power. I was the cowboy, Zoe was my "girl," the boys we knew were Indians. I was the detective, Zoe was my "girl," the boys were the robbers. I was Peter Pan, Zoe was Wendy Darling, the boys were the lost boys. And the terrain around the river—jungled and dark green—was Tombstone or Chicago or Never-Never-Land.

This place and my friendship with Zoe never touched my life in Kingston. We did not correspond with each other when I left my grandmother's home.

I never visited Zoe's home the entire time I knew her. It was a given: never suggested, never raised.

Zoe went to a state school held in a country church in Red Hills. It had been my mother's school. I went to a private all-girls school where I was taught by white Englishwomen and pale Jamaicans. In her school the students were caned as punishment. In mine the harshest punishment I remember was being sent to sit under the *lignum vitae* to "commune with nature." Some of the girls were out-and-out white (English and American), the rest of us were colored—only a few were dark. Our uniforms were blood-red gabardine, heavy and hot. Classes were held in buildings meant to recreate England: damp with stone floors, facing onto a cloister, or quad as they called it. We began each day with the headmistress leading us in English hymns. The entire school stood for an hour in the zinc-roofed gymnasium.

Occasionally a girl fainted, or threw up. Once, a girl had a grand mal seizure. To any such disturbance the response was always "keep singing." While she flailed on the stone floor, I wondered what the mistresses would do. We sang "Faith of Our Fathers" and watched our classmate as her eyes rolled back in her head. I thought of people swallowing their tongues. The student was dark—here on a scholarship—and the only woman who came forward to help her was the gamesmistress, the only dark teacher. She kneeled beside the girl and slid the white web belt from her tennis shorts, clamping it between the girl's teeth. When the seizure was over, she carried the girl to a tumbling mat in a corner of the gym and covered her so she wouldn't get chilled.

Were the other women unable to touch this girl because of her darkness? I think so now. Her darkness and her scholarship. She lived on Windward Road with her grandmother; her mother was a live-in maid. But darkness is usually enough for women like those to hold back. Then, we usually excused that kind of behavior by saying they were "ladies." (We were constantly being told we should be ladies also. One teacher went so far as to tell us many people thought Jamaicans lived in trees, and we had to show these people they were mistaken.) In short, we felt insufficient to judge the behavior of these women. The English ones (the ones who had the corner on power in the school) had come all this way to teach us. Shouldn't we treat them as the missionaries they were certain they were? The creole Jamaicans had a different role: they were passing on to those of us who were light-skinned the creole heritage of collaboration, assimilation, loyalty to our betters. We were expected to be willing subjects in this outpost of civilization.

The girl left school that day and never returned.

After prayers we filed into our classrooms. After classes we had games: tennis, field hockey, rounders (what the English call baseball), netball (what the English call basketball). For games we were divided into "houses"—groups named for Joan of Arc, Edith Cavell, Florence Nightingale, Jane Austen. Four white heroines. Two martyrs. One saint. Two nurses. (None of us knew that there were Black women with Nightingale at Scutari.) One novelist. Three involved in white men's wars. Two dead in white men's wars. *Pride and Prejudice.*

Those of us in Cavell wore red badges and recited her last words before a firing squad in W. W. I: "Patriotism is not enough. I must have no hatred or bitterness toward anyone."

Sorry to say I grew up to have exactly that.

Looking back: To try and see where the background changed places with the foreground. To try and locate the vanishing point: where lines of perspective converge and disappear. Lines of color and class. Lines of history and social context. Lines of denial and rejection. When did *we,* the light-skinned middle-class Jamaicans, take over for *them* as oppressors? I need to see how and when this happened. When what should have been reality was taken over by what was surely unreality. When the house nigger became master.

"What's the matter with you? You think you're white or something?"
"Child, what you want to know 'bout Garvey for? The man was nothing but a damn fool."
"They not our kind of people."

Why did we wear wide-brimmed hats and try to get into Oxford?
Why did we not return?

Great Expectations: a novel about origins and denial, about the futil-
ity and tragedy of that denial, about attempting assimilation. We
learned this novel from a light-skinned Jamaican woman—she
concentrated on what she called the "love affair" between Pip and
Estella.

Looking back: Through the last page of *Sula.* "And the loss pressed
down on her chest and came up into her throat. 'We was girls
together,' she said as though explaining something." It was Zoe,
and Zoe alone, I thought of. She snapped into my mind, and I
remembered no one else. Through the greens and blues of the riv-
erbank. The flame of red hibiscus in front of my grandmother's
house. The cracked grave of a former landowner. The fruit of the
ackee, which poisons those who don't know how to prepare it.

"What is to become of us?"
We borrowed a baby from a woman and used her as our dolly.
Dressed and undressed her. Dipped her in the riverwater. Fed her
with the milk her mother had left with us: and giggled because
we knew where the milk had come from.

A letter: "I am desperate. I need to get away. I beg you one fifty
dollar."

I send her money because this is what she asks for. I visit her on
a trip back home. Her front teeth are gone. Her husband beats

her and she suffers blackouts. I sit on her chair. She is given birth control pills, which aggravate her "condition." We boil up sorrel and ginger. She is being taught by the Peace Corps volunteers to embroider linen mats with little lambs on them and gives me one as a keepsake. We cool off the sorrel with a block of ice brought from the shop nearby. The shopkeeper immediately recognizes me as my grandmother's granddaughter and refuses to sell me cigarettes. (I am twenty-seven.) We sit in the doorway of her house, pushing back the colored plastic strands which form a curtain, and talk about Babylon and Dred. About Manley and what he's doing for Jamaica. About how hard it is. We walk along the railway tracks—no longer used—to Crooked River and the post office. Her little daughter walks beside us, and we recite a poem for her: "Mornin' buddy/Me no buddy fe wunna/Who den, den I saw?" and on and on.

I can come and go. And I leave. To complete my education in London.

II

Their goddam kings and their goddam queens. Grandmotherly Victoria spreading herself thin across the globe. Elizabeth II on our tv screens. We stop what we are doing. We quiet down. We pay our respects.

1981: In Massachusetts I get up at 5 a.m. to watch the royal wedding. I tell myself maybe the IRA will intervene. It's got to be better than starving themselves to death. Better to be a kamikaze in

St. Paul's Cathedral than a hostage in Ulster. And last week Black and white people smashed storefronts all over the United Kingdom. But I don't really believe we'll see royal blood on tv. I watch because they once ruled us. In the back of the cathedral a Maori woman sings an aria from Handel, and I notice that she is surrounded by the colored subjects.

To those of us in the Commonwealth the royal family was the perfect symbol of hegemony. To those of us who were dark in the dark nations, the prime minister, the parliament barely existed. We believed in royalty—we were convinced in this belief. Maybe it played on some ancestral memories of West Africa—of other kings and queens. Altars and castles and magic.

The faces of our new rulers were everywhere in my childhood. Calendars, newsreels, magazines. Their presences were often among us. Attending test matches between the West Indians and South Africans. They were our landlords. Not always absentee. And no matter what Black leader we might elect—were we to choose independence—we would be losing something almost holy in our impudence.

> **WE ARE HERE BECAUSE YOU WERE THERE**
> **BLACK PEOPLE AGAINST STATE BRUTALITY**
> **BLACK WOMEN WILL NOT BE INTIMIDATED**
> **WELCOME TO BRITAIN . . .**
> **WELCOME TO SECOND-CLASS CITIZENSHIP.**
> (slogans of the Black movement in Britain)

Indian women cleaning the toilets in Heathrow Airport. This is the first thing I notice. Dark women in saris trudging buckets back and forth as other dark women in saris—some covered by loose-fitting winter coats—form a line to have their passports stamped. Reinforcements.

The triangle trade: molasses/rum/slaves. Robinson Crusoe was on a slave-trading journey. Robert Browning was a mulatto. Holding pens. Jamaica was a seasoning station. Split tongues. Sliced ears. Whipped bodies. The constant pretense of civility against rape. Still. Iron collars. Tinplate masks. The latter a precaution: to stop the slaves from eating the sugar cane. Under the tropic sun, faces cooked.

A pregnant woman is to be whipped—they dig a hole to accommodate her belly and place her facedown on the ground. Many of us became light-skinned very fast. Traced ourselves through bastard lines to reach the duke of Devonshire. The earl of Cornwall. The lord of this and the lord of that. Our mothers' rapes were the things unspoken.

You say: But Britain freed her slaves in 1833. Yes.

Tea plantations in India and Ceylon. Mines in Africa. The Cape-to-Cairo Railroad. Rhodes scholars. Suez Crisis. The white man's bloody burden. Boer War. Bantustans. Sitting in a theatre in London in the seventies. A play called *West of Suez*. A lousy play about British colonials. The finale comes when several well-known white actors are machine-gunned by several lesser-known Black actors. (As Nina Simone says: "This is a show tune but the show hasn't been written for it yet.")

The red empire of geography classes. "The sun never sets on the British Empire and you can't trust it in the dark." Or with dark peoples. "Because of the Industrial Revolution European countries went in search of markets and raw materials." Another geography (or was it a history) lesson.

Their bloody kings and their bloody queens. Their bloody peers. Their bloody generals. Admirals. Explorers. Livingstone. Hillary. Kitchener. All the bwanas. And all their beaters, porters, sherpas. Who found the source of the Nile. Victoria Falls. The tops of mountains. The roof of the world. Their so-called discoveries reek of untruth. How many dark people died so they could misname the physical features in their blasted gazetteer. A statistic we shall never know. Dr. Livingstone, I presume you are here to rape our land and enslave our people.

There are statues of these dead white men all over London.

An interesting fact: The swear word "bloody" is a contraction of "by my lady"—a reference to the Virgin Mary. They do tend to use their ladies. Name ages for them. Places for them. Use them as screens, inspirations, symbols. And many of the ladies comply. While the national martyr Edith Cavell was being executed by the Germans in 1915 in Belgium (called "poor little Belgium" by the allies in the war), the Belgians were engaged in the exploitation of the land and peoples of the Congo—actually decimation.

And will we ever know how many dark peoples were imported to fight in white men's wars. Probably not. Just as we will never know how many hearts were cut from African people so that the Christian doctor might be a success—i.e., extend a white man's life. Our Sister Killjoy observes this from her black-eyed squint—no sweetness here.

Dr. Schweitzer—humanitarian, authority on Bach, winner of the Nobel Peace Prize—on the people of his adopted continent: "The Negro is a child, and with children nothing can be done without the use of authority. We must, therefore, so arrange the circumstances of our daily life that my authority can find expression. With Negroes, then, I have coined the formula: 'I am your brother, it is true, but your elder brother'" (*On the Edge of the Primeval Forest,* 1961).

They like to pretend we didn't fight back. We did: with obeah, poison, revolution. It simply was not enough.

"Colonies . . . these places where 'niggers' are cheap and the earth is rich" (W. E. B. DuBois, "The Souls of White Folk," 1910).

A cousin is visiting me from Caltech where he is getting a degree in engineering. I am learning about the Italian Renaissance. My cousin is recognizably Black and speaks with an accent. I am not and do not—unless I am back home, where the twang comes upon me. We sit for some time in a bar in his hotel and are not served. A light-skinned Jamaican comes over to our table. He is an older man—a professor at the University of London. "Don't bother with it, you hear. They don't serve us in this bar." A run-of-the-mill incident for all recognizably Black people in this city. But for me it is not.

Henry's eyes fill up, but he refuses to believe our informant. "No, man, the girl is just busy." (The girl is a fifty-year-old white woman, who may just be following orders. But I do not mention this. I have chosen sides.) All I can manage to say is, "Jesus Christ, I hate the fucking English." Henry looks at me. (In the family I am known as the "lady cousin." It has to do with how I look. And the fact that I am twenty-seven and unmarried—and for all they know, unattached. They do not know that I am really the lesbian cousin. Not yet.) Our informant says—gently, but with a distinct tone of disappointment—"My dear, is that what you are studying at the university?"

You see, the whole business is very complicated.

Henry and I leave without drinks and go to meet some of his white colleagues at a restaurant I know near Covent Garden Opera House. The restaurant caters to theatre types, and so I hope there won't be a repeat of the bar scene—at least they know how to pretend. Besides, I tell myself, the owners are Italian *and* gay; they *must* be halfway decent. Henry and his colleagues work for an American company which is paying their way through Caltech. They mine bauxite from the hills in the middle of the island and send it to the United States. A turnaround occurs at dinner: Henry joins the white men in a sustained mockery of the waiters: their accents and their mannerisms. He whispers to me: "Why you want to bring us to a battyman den, lady?" (*Battyman* = *faggot* in Jamaican) I keep quiet.

We put the whitemen in a taxi, and Henry walks me to the Underground station. He asks me to sleep with him. "Cousin pot boil the sweetest soup," he says. (It wouldn't be incest, not really. His mother was a maid in the house of an uncle, and Henry has not seen her since his birth. He was taken into the family. She was let go.) I say that I can't. I plead exams. I can't say that I don't want to. Because I remember what happened in the bar. But I can't say that I'm a lesbian either—even though I want to believe his alliance with the white men at dinner was forced, not really him. He doesn't buy my excuse. "Come on, lady, let's do it. What's the matter, you 'fraid?" I pretend I am back home and start *patois* to show him somehow I am not afraid, not English, not white. I tell him he's a married man, and he tells me he's a ram goat. I take the train to where I am staying and try to forget the whole thing. But I cannot. I remember our different skins and our different experiences within them. And I have a hard time realizing that I am angry at Henry. That to him—no use in pretending—a queer is a queer.

1981: I hear on the radio that Bob Marley is dead, and I drive over the Mohawk Trail, listening to a program of his music, and I cry and cry and cry. Someone says: "It wasn't the ganja that killed him, it was poverty and working in a steel foundry when he was young."

I flash back to my childhood and a young man who worked for a relative I lived with once. He taught me to smoke ganja behind the house. And to peel an orange with the tip of a machete without cutting through the skin—"Love" it was called; a necklace of orange rind the result. I think about him because I heard he had become a Rastaman. And then I think about Rastas.

We are sitting on the porch of an uncle's house in Kingston—the family and I—and a Rastaman comes to the gate. We have guns but they are locked behind a false closet. We have dogs but they are tied up. We are Jamaicans and know that Rastas mean no harm. We let him in and he sits on the side of the porch and shows us his brooms and brushes. We buy some to take back to New York. "Peace, missis."

There were many Rastas in my childhood. Walking the roadside with their goods. Sitting outside their shacks in the mountains. The outsides painted as bright as the pirogues that line Kingston Harbour. Sometimes with words. Rastas gathering at Palisadoes Airport to greet the Conquering Lion of Judah. They were considered figures of fun by most middle-class Jamaicans. Harmless—like Marcus Garvey.

Later: white American hippies trying to create the effect of dred in their straight white hair. The ganja joint held between their straight white teeth. "Man, the grass is good." Hanging out by the Sheraton, haunting the white sands of Negril. Light-skinned Jamaicans also assuming the spliff. Both groups moving to the music but not the words. Harmless. "Peace, brother."

III

My mother's mother: "Let us thank God for a fruitful place."
My mother's father: "Let us rescue the perishing world."

This evening on the road in western Massachusetts there are pockets of fog. Then clear spaces. Across from a pond a dog staggers in front of my headlights. I look closer and see that his mouth is foaming. He stumbles to the side of the road. I go to call the police.

I drive back to the house, radio playing "difficult" piano pieces. And I think about how I need to say all this. This is who I am. I am not what you allow me to be. Whatever you decide me to be. In a bookstore in London I show the woman at the counter my book, and she stares at me for a minute, then says: "You're a Jamaican." "Yes." "You're not at all like our Jamaicans."

Encountering the void is nothing more nor less than understanding invisibility. Of being fogbound.

Then:
It was never a question of passing. It was a question of hiding. Behind Black and white perceptions of who we were—who they thought we were. Tropics. Plantations. Calypso. Cricket. We were the people with the musical voices and the coronation mugs on our parlor tables. I would be whatever figurine these foreign imaginations cared for me to be. It would be so simple to let others fill in for me. So easy to startle them with a flash of anger when their visions got out of hand—but never to sustain the anger for myself. It could be a life lived within myself. A life cut off. I know who I am but you will never know who I am. I may in fact lose touch with who I am.

I hid from my true sources. But my true sources were also hidden from me.

Now:

It is not a question of relinquishing privilege. It is a question of grasping more of myself. I have found that in the true sources are concealed my survival. My speech. My voice. To be colonized is to be rendered insensible. To have those parts necessary to sustain life numbed. And this is in some cases—in my case—perceived as privilege. The test of a colonized person is to walk through a shantytown in Kingston and not bat an eye. This I cannot do. Because part of me lives there—and as I grasp more of this part I realize what needs to be done with the rest of my life.

Sometimes I used to think we were like the Marranos—the Sephardic Jews forced to pretend they were Christians. The name was given to them by the Christians; it meant "pigs." But once out of Spain and Portugal, they became Jews openly again. Some settled in Jamaica. They knew who the enemy was and acted for their own survival. But they remained Jews always.

We also knew who the enemy was—I remember jokes about the English. Saying they stank. saying they were stingy. that they drank too much and couldn't hold their liquor. that they had bad teeth. were dirty and dishonest. were limey bastards. and horse-faced bitches. We said the men only wanted to sleep with Jamaican women. And that Englishwomen made pigs of themselves with Jamaican men.

But of course this was seen by us—the light-skinned middle class—with a double vision. We learned to cherish that part of us that was them, and to deny the part that was not. Believing in some cases that the latter part had ceased to exist.

None of this is as simple as it sounds. We were colorists and we aspired to oppressor status. (Of course, almost any aspiration instilled by Western civilization is to oppressor status: success, for example.) Color was the symbol of our potential: color taking in hair "quality," skin tone, freckles, nose width, eyes. We did not see that color symbolism was a method of keeping us apart: in the society, in the family, between friends. Those of us who were light-skinned, straight-haired, etc., were given to believe that we could actually attain whiteness—at least those qualities of the colonizer that rendered him superior. We were convinced of white supremacy. If we failed in our quest, we were not really responsible for our failure: we had all the advantages—but that one persistent drop of blood, that single rogue gene that made us unable to conceptualize abstract ideas, made us love darkness rather than despise it, was to be blamed for our failure. Our dark part had taken over: an inherited imbalance in which the doom of the creole was sealed.

I am trying to write this as clearly as possible, but as I write I realize that what I say may sound fabulous, or even mythic. It is. It is insane.

Under this system of colorism—the system which prevailed in my childhood in Jamaica and which has carried over to the present—rarely will dark and light people co-mingle. Rarely will they achieve between themselves an intimacy informed with identity.

(I should say here that I am using the categories light and dark both literally and symbolically. There are dark Jamaicans who have achieved lightness and the "advantages" which go with it by their successful pursuit of oppressor status.)

Under this system light and dark people will meet in those ways in which the light-skinned person imitates the oppressor. But imitation goes only so far: the light-skinned person becomes an oppressor in fact. He or she will have a dark chauffeur, a dark nanny, a dark maid, and a dark gardener. These employees will be paid badly. Because of the slave past, because of their dark skin which links them to that past, the servants of the middle class have been used according to the traditions of the slavocracy. They are not seen as workers for their own sake but for the sake of the family that has employed them. It was not until Michael Manley became prime minister that a minimum wage for houseworkers was enacted—and the indignation of the middle class was profound.

During Manley's leadership the middle class began to abandon the island in droves. Toronto. Miami. New York. Leaving their houses and businesses behind and sewing cash into the tops of suitcases. Today—with a new regime (in thrall to the CIA)—they are returning. "Come back to the way things used to be," the tourist advertisement on American tv says. "Make it Jamaica again. Make it your own."

But let me return to the situation of houseservants as I remember it: They will be paid badly, but they will be "given" room and board. However, the key to the larder will be kept by the mistress in her dresser drawer. They will spend Christmas with the family of their employers and be given a length of English wool for trousers or a few yards of sea island cotton for a dress. They will see their children on their days off; their extended family will care for the children the rest of the time. When the employers visit their relations in the country, the servants may be asked along—oftentimes the servants of the middle class come from the same part of the countryside their employers have come from. But they will be expected to work while they are there. Back in town, there are parts of the house they are allowed to move freely around; other parts they are not allowed to enter. When the family watches the tv, the servant is allowed to watch also, but only while standing in a doorway. The servant may have a radio in his/her room, also a dresser and a cot. Perhaps a mirror. There will usually be one ceiling light. And one small square louvered window.

A true story: One middle-class Jamaican woman ordered a Persian rug from Harrods in London. The day it arrived, so did her new maid. She was going downtown to have her hair touched up, and told the maid to vacuum the rug. She told the maid she would find the vacuum cleaner in the same shed as the power mower. And when she returned she found that the fine nap of her new rug had been removed. The labor of tiny fingers decimated.

The reaction of the mistress was to tell her friends that the "girl" was backward. She did not fire her until she found that the maid had scrubbed the Teflon from her new set of pots, saying she thought they were coated with "nastiness."

The houseworker/mistress relationship in which one Black woman is the oppressor of another Black woman is a cornerstone of the experience of many Jamaican women.

I recall another true story: In a middle-class family's home one Christmas, a relation was visiting from New York. This woman had brought gifts for everybody, including the housemaid. The maid had been released from a mental institution recently, where they had treated her for depression. This visiting light-skinned woman had brought the dark woman a bright red rayon blouse and presented it to her in the garden one afternoon, while the family was having tea. The maid thanked her softly, and the visitor moved toward her as if to embrace her. Then she stopped, her face suddenly covered with tears, and ran into the house, saying, "My God, I can't, I can't."

We are women who come from a place almost incredible in its beauty. A beauty which can mask a great deal and which has been used in that way. But that the beauty is there is a fact. I remember what I thought the freedom of my childhood, in which the fruitful place was something I took for granted. Just as I took for granted Zoe's appearance every morning on my school vacations—in the sense that I knew she would always be the one to visit me. The perishing world of my grandfather's graces at the table, if I ever seriously thought about it, was somewhere else.

Our souls were affected by the beauty of Jamaica, as much as they were affected by our fears of darkness.

There is no ending to this piece of writing. There is no way I can end it. As I read back over it, I see that we/they/I may become confused in the mind of the reader: but these pronouns have always coexisted in my mind. The Rastafarians talk of the "I and I"—a pronoun in which they combine themselves with Jah. Jah is a contraction of Jahweh and Jehovah, but to me always sounds like the beginning of Jamaica. I and Jamaica is who I am. No matter how far I travel—how deep the ambivalence I feel about ever returning. And Jamaica is a place in which we/they/I connect and disconnect—change place.

Cross-Country:
A Documentary in Ten Jump-Cuts

I

I head through the mountains past the Tehachapi Loop, descend into the Mojave, blasting the speed limit, past proving grounds, the landscape like every fifties horror movie I remember. *Fiend without a Face.* I stop in Barstow, which looks like the town in *D.O.A.* (noncolorized).

I am almost alone on the road, Verdi's *Otello* on the tape deck.

The opera now over, I scan the dial but can raise only a few AM stations. A born-again-just-say-no radio play comes on, complete with organ and resonant male voice. The passage of time, the wages of sin. I am sucked back, somewhere, door slamming, feet rushing, water running. I am in a pitch-black room, in bed with measles, the radio tuned to *The Romance of Helen Trent.*

"There *is* an entrance exam for Heaven," the voice intones.

I am saved (but not in his sense) by Lacy J. Dalton, as stations slide over and under each other. "Black coffee/blue mornin'/toast is burnin'/rain keeps fallin'/sad feelin'/I'm losin' you."

I stop at a place at the side of the road hysterical with signs. Over the door, over the gas pumps, on the way in, on the way out, over the condom machine in the ladies' room.

LAST GAS FOR 100 MILES   LAST CHANCE UNTIL NEEDLES
NO WATER UNTIL THE COLORADO

YOU ARE HERE   A pin is stuck in the middle of a blank sheet of paper.

At the side of the road several miles beyond is a suitcase. Just sitting there. Upright. An old-fashioned striped valise. Traveling salesman's case? Runaway from a nursing home? The thing haunts me.

I cross the Colorado and begin to climb in Arizona. The temperature drops and the sun begins to set. Ice glints on the highway where tamaracks cast their shadows.

I put on *Tosca* with Callas, and try to calm myself, which, if you think about it, is silly. Cold and icy, and the road continues upward. Tosca's kiss. Dark now. Passing semis send cascades of ice and salt over my car. There is nothing anywhere.

Then: finally: oasis. A motel rises from the snow at the side of the highway. As snowbound as the Overlook, as isolated as the Bates—I don't care. I don't care if there are stuffed birds in the lobby, a maze in the parking lot. I check in, have my dream American meal: steak, rare, baked potato, Wild Turkey and water. I am amused by my own predictability.

The next day: 9 below.

In the coffee shop at the motel are kachina dolls. Sacred as kitsch. The waitresses are native women. We are at the edge of the Navaho Reservation, south of the Grand Canyon, in a town named for a trailblazer.

The manager is telling a waitress, "He's no good for you." She nods. Looks down. I stare into my food.

As I prepare to leave, my car dies. It is revived by a man whose thirty-fifth birthday this is. He tells me he's worried he won't be able to satisfy his twenty-three-year-old wife much longer. I try to reassure him.

He teaches me how to fix a carburetor at high altitudes, in cold weather: always travel with a clothespin.

He drives away, his gold earring glinting against the clean blue-white of the snow.

I head in the direction of Albuquerque.

I begin to relax as I descend, leaving the ice behind.

Painted Desert. Petrified Forest.

Petroglyphs. Faces. Ears. Birds. Snakes. Newspaper Rock.

Wigwam Motel. "Sleep in an air-conditioned wigwam."

The edges of reservations.

Sky City of the Acoma.

Nearby the I.H.S. Hospital. Has anyone noted the irony in those initials?

Gallup. OLD TIME INDIAN PAWN JEWELRY. Over and over and again. Pawnshops alternate with liquor stores.

Men and women stagger along the streets. Live from Gallup, it's Saturday afternoon.

Sunday morning: men and women with battered faces hitch rides back to the reservation.

Albuquerque to Amarillo.

Billboard: faded: rattlesnake egg inside glass paperweight.

As soon as I cross into Texas, the terrain changes.

Ancient hand-lettered sign posted on the flat flat land:

> STOP HELPING COMMUNISM
> HERE
> THERE
> EVERYWHERE

A last-picture-show town at first glance, complete with old cowboy inside the filling station, sitting in an easy chair by the space heater, sipping a Coca-Cola.

On his radio an ad for "Bubba's Barbecue," with a recipe for sauce "brought all the way from Virginia by Bubba's people." Juneteenth.

Oklahoma:

HITCHHIKERS MAY BE ESCAPING INMATES

I cross into Missouri on the anniversary of Elvis's birthday.

Spend the night in Joplin. The motel is across from a place calling itself "Fag Bearings."

I turn on the tv and watch a "life" of Rock Hudson. Dreadful. Fag bearings indeed. Apparently two men can be shown in bed together only when one of them has night sweats.

The Copper something. A HoJo restaurant in a little town in the Ozarks. I've had too much red meat en route. Need, crave, plain white food. Turkey on white bread with mayonnaise.

I am sitting at the counter. The windows at one side of the room hold a spectacular view of the mountains. A young woman a few stools away is talking to herself, so it seems. Wearing a red beret, drinking black coffee, chain-smoking. I don't see the baby in her lap. She seems shaky, talking a mile a minute. Talking now to the waitress who doesn't pay her a lot of mind but who smiles and keeps the refills coming.

The young woman asks no one in particular, "How are things in Florida?"

She says, again to no one in particular, "I just can't afford day care." She seems to be anticipating something. She says, now directly to the waitress who is standing in front of her: "There was a real soap opera this morning in number six." The waitress, also a very young woman, nods. The speaker continues: "She just got herself a job and then didn't want to go to it. So he let her have it."

My sandwich arrives and with it a young man with hieroglyphics on his arms. He's the cook. Lanky, with tinted glasses, a sallow face. He's smiling, showing poor people's teeth. It turns out the young woman in the beret (the beret and the jaunty red of it haunts me, the way she wore it tilted to one side) is married to him.

She speaks again, and with this I finally realize she has a baby in her lap, who has been absolutely silent.

"I don't care if he's a baseball player or a football player, as long as he's happy."

The baby is lifted out of her lap by the young man. He's pale and skinny, a baby the social worker might cite for "failure to thrive."

He's dandled and played with while the young woman starts speaking even more rapidly. She's saying she's cleaned the place, and "there ain't no more trash anywhere."

The cook whispers back at her, what I cannot hear.

Her response is urgent. She reassures him over and over that the trash has been removed, the place cleaned, and the landlady won't be able to do anything.

The cook returns to the kitchen, and she continues, speaking into the air.

"How are things in Florida?"

I get in my car and drive away.

I pass through St. Louis, think of Josephine Baker, escaping.

The red beret returns to me. I cannot forget her; I never will.

II

I am on my way to the University of Virginia.

I cross the Hudson at the Fishkill Correctional Facility, which I mistake for Sing Sing.

As I drive this country, I become aware of places where people are kept, begin to guess them from a distance, the state-of-the-art, the ancient.

At the side of the highway are huge rolls of barbed wire, like baled hay.

I recall when I saw San Quentin at night. A wrong turn on the way to the Pacific Ocean, and then the lit-up Oz, yellow-green in the bay fog. A Friday night, and scores of dressed-up women were leaving the prison, walking toward a line of buses. I parked and went inside to ask directions. I noticed a sign saying "San Quentin Gift Shop" hanging above a guard's head. Even he was washed in the yellow-green light.

I am driving past the coal mines of eastern Pennsylvania. Like the salt mines of Detroit, the refineries of New Jersey, small houses, clotheslines, gardens, bang up against them.

Slag heaps stand like monuments.

From the heights of the Alleghenies I descend into the terrain of farmland, battlefield.

Every few miles or so, this happens about three times, are three crosses—life-size—at the side of the road. The thieves' are yellow, the centerpiece blue.

Nearing Gettysburg, I pass a truck from the Fort Sumter Casket Company.

I spend the night in Hagerstown, Maryland. The young man from room service comes in. *Shadow of a Doubt* is playing on the tv. "That's another thing with those old movies," he says, as Teresa Wright accepts her Uncle Charlie's ring, lifted from the finger of a murdered "merry widow." "The ladies were beautiful and they were good women."

I am close to Antietam Battlefield. Gospel from D.C. is playing on the radio. "Blessed assurance, Jesus is mine." The d.j. cuts in, apologizes for playing Pat Boone, saying she wanted "to give the boy a chance, but enough is enough."

I turn the car into a road that runs through the battlefield. It is early morning. A mist hangs over aisles of corn. Cows graze, stroll through grass, lush from the potash, from the human remains underneath. The same farmhouses, barns as in 1862. I pick up a stone, witness, pocket it. The past closes in behind my eyes. I have seen photographs of that day and recognize the ditch where the bodies were stacked like cordwood when the day was over. I walk through the ditch. Blackbirds pick over last year's cornstalks. Pick through the ground. There is the sound of a mockingbird, his musical shuttle. Behind that the hum of cars in the early morning, Saturday, on a secondary road in the Maryland countryside.

Not all were left on the battlefield. In a graveyard in Sharpsburg are row on row of tiny white headstones. The word *unknown* repeats and repeats so many times as to become meaningless.

At the University of Virginia I am informed (by the doctoral student who is my escort) that Thomas Jefferson didn't own slaves, news to me. "Villagers"—as they're affectionately known—built the university, Monticello, every rotunda, column, and finial the great man dreamed of. They liked him so much they just pitched in, after their own chores were done. She tells me all this with a straight face. I ask her about Sally Hemings, the slave who bore Jefferson several children. I am told she did not exist; if she did, she was white. History as fiction.

I cannot resist: I ask her if she's ever met a white person named Jefferson, or Washington for that matter.

III

San Jose Airport. I am in line at American Airlines. An extremely old man stands behind me. Immense eyebrows shade his eyes. He is familiar. I realize that he's Edward Teller. An old man leaning on a Margaret Mead–style walking stick. People offer to help him with his bags, but he ignores them. Soon enough he realizes he's in the wrong line and moves over to first class.

IV

New York City. I am here for a conference on multiculturalism. They've put us up in one of those renovated old hotels. This one in the thirties at Madison Avenue. The Martha Washington is around the block, where—I remember this from high school—Veronica Lake was found working as a chambermaid. It made headlines: A STAR'S DISGRACE etc.

All the boys and girls who came from somewhere else. Like D., who came to the City in the 1940s with her trumpet, not realizing there wasn't much call for lady horn players, Boston Brahmin at that, nor Black from Chicago, for that matter—or perhaps knowing, and hoping against hope to become the exception. The halls of the old hotel immediately become a black-and-white movie, in the rooms, Murphy bed, hot plate, clothesline stretched from wall to wall, but the bliss of independence the true prize, the knowledge of having left the place of suffocation behind.

I walk through a New York City downpour. An old man says to me: "In weather like this, honey, all you can do is sing." I laugh and join him in a chorus of "It Had to Be You," half-expecting strings, a chorus, fade to black.

At Columbus Circle, under the overhang of the Coliseum, is a single bed, made with a baby-blue blanket, accumulating sweat from the rain, tidy as an ad in *Woman's Day*.

Back at the hotel a wedding party clogs the dining room at breakfast. So much hairspray and perfume in the air it's like being "trapped in the revolving doors at Bloomingdale's"—so says the maître d', gay émigré from Louisville.

The conference is relatively uneventful, unimaginative: discourse, hegemonic, gendered, privilege—all the academic lingo the participants can muster is thrown about, so affrighted they seem by imaginations entirely foreign to them, beyond their control. One critic calls the Third World "postcolonial" and a writer from Ghana calls that "a sadistic joke."

I leave the City to a tribute to Sarah Vaughan.

V

I am driving along a secondary road beside Lake Erie on a Sunday afternoon in May. High, soft clouds overhead. My eye

catches a sign, handpainted, in earth colors, at the side of the road:
WELCOME TO TOUSSAINT COUNTRY   Nothing else   Or did it say
TOUSSAINT COUNTY?

Either way my heart jumps. Did some of C. L. R. James's
Black Jacobins end up here?

Possible.

Jamaican slaves ended up in Nova Scotia. The recalcitrant and
trouble-making ones.

Why not Haitians in Ohio?

VI

I am in Omaha, in an old brick building on the black side of
town. Around the building are small tidy houses, vegetable and
flower gardens, lilacs in bud, rhubarb stalks beginning to redden,
tulips just about finished. Housedresses, overalls, undershirts,
nightgowns flap in the breezes of the Great Plains, off the Missouri River. On the street are debris of rusted cars, and a beat-up
place with the "best barbecue in Omaha" has ceased to exist.

A woman, disheveled, crack-skinny, runs in front of my car
screaming "Bitch!"

A casualty of our forgetfulness.

The brick building is the Great Plains Black Museum, in this
town where Malcolm X was born. The rooms of the museum are
packed. A son's graduation portrait from West Point. Buffalo soldiers on duty at Fort Robinson. Witnesses to the death of Crazy
Horse.

A woman in a high-neck collar, her hair upswept with tortoise-
shell combs. A man in a high-neck collar with a watch fob across
his vest. Tuskegee airmen. A woman named Liza Suggs who

recorded her family's escape from slavery. Inhabitants of Brownlee and Brownville, all-black towns in Nebraska. The epitaph of Ben Hodges:

SELF-STYLED DESPERADO
A COLORFUL PIONEER
1856–1929

Upstairs a pioneer dwelling has been re-created. Quilts, canned goods, recipes, home remedies, iron bedstead. I try to imagine the people who put this food by, who passed through the phases of human life on this bedstead, under this quilt. I pass my hand across the label on a Mason jar holding strawberry jam.

In the basement a figure in an Olympic warm-up suit raises a black-gloved fist. Newspapers from 1919 lie on a table next to the black Olympian.

LYNCHING   RIOTS   RACE
RED SUMMER
RIOTING   RACE   LYNCHING ELUDED
RIOTING   RACE   RACE
RACE   WAR HERO
LYNCHING

The head-and-shoulders mannequin from the window of a beauty parlor stands to one side. On one copper shoulder is inscribed LADY DAY 1915–1959: I think back to the woman on the street.

VII

Farther west. Fronts are flying across the landscape. Hail and wind rock the car. I put the pedal to the metal and can only do 55.

A woman is squatting on an island in the middle of the interstate, laughing, the wind whipping her against the divider.

As soon as one front passes, another is visible on the horizon.

A tumbleweed gets caught in my antenna, and I start to sing, "A tumbleweed got caught in my antenna, as I drove my way back to you."

I pull off the road at Little America, get out to hailstones pounding the car, the wind is boundless. I get lunch, then browse through the gift shop, filled with people who look like they're old hands at this.

"Just pray we don't have to hit the ditch," one woman says, laughing.

I delay my departure by looking in the glass cases. Hats with rattlesnake heads, fangs bared. A bin of arrowheads. Soapstone carvings. A plaque with six kinds of barbed wire: THE WIRE THAT FENCED THE WEST.

I decide I'm being chicken and leave.

I finally seem to be in the rhythm of the weather, exhilarated at eluding the funnel clouds winding their way across the interstate.

At Salt Lake City the skies turn pitch, and open, rain pounding the Great Salt Lake, water lapping at the side of the highway and the salt glistens white against skies as black as space.

VIII

Ahead: Nevada. I can see sunlight. Winnemucca. I go into a liquor store and find that there are several shelves of fine porcelain figurines — of the sort that might decorate a mantelpiece in a Willa Cather novel. I ask the young woman behind the counter what these figurines represent—all are female. "Oh, those are the famous whores of Nevada." One is particularly striking—a woman dressed in a schoolmarmish floor-length skirt and long-sleeved blouse, standing next to a railing with a firehat on it. She is identified to me as Julia Bullette, known as a "public woman." I purchase the figurine as well as a booklet describing her life.

Julia Bullette was a citizen of Virginia City during the Comstock silver boom. Self-employed, well respected, and an honorary fireman—Liberty Engine Company 1—hence the helmet. She was murdered by a man named Jean A. Villain, who cut her throat as she slept—January 20, 1867. Mark Twain attended his hanging.

Back at the hotel CNN is following the Simpson trial. The jury is still out.

IX

Pittsburgh, Fall 2001.
Without Sanctuary (Images of Lynching at the Warhol Museum). Amidst the silence of elongated black bodies is Cattle Kate—a full-face photo of her in "happier times." And with the photo, this poem, unsigned:

> Some boys in Deadwood asked again:
> "You knew her once, didn't you Ben?"
> "Well, yes," I said. That's all I said.
> Then rode on down toward Lead.
> The wind blew through those Black Hills flowers
> One Spring day. The sun shone on our heads.
> I'll pack my Colts and board a train
> For old Wyoming once again.

To even up the score for Kate.
No man can change his fate.
Snow blows through the Black Hills towers
But did I say: "The sun shone on our heads?"

On All Saints' Day, 2001, a woman is walking down S. Craig Street. She is wearing a long floral granny dress and has dirty blonde hair to her shoulders. She is pushing a stroller with an American flag taped to one handle. A black woman approaching her looks into the stroller and does a double take worthy of Lou Costello.

On the Day of the Dead, 2001, I am sitting in the Union Grill on S. Craig Street when a woman walks in pushing a stroller with an American flag taped to one handle. She sits at a table across from me and removes from the stroller a life-size baby doll, which she feeds, changes, rocks, and sings to sleep. Of course I remember the red beret in the Ozarks, link these two in my mind.

December 15, 2001: An article in the *Post-Gazette* tells of a box of human remains from the 1950s that has been kept in a sheriff's office in western Pennsylvania—unidentified and unclaimed. The body—a male about thirty or so—was found by two hunters during deer-hunting season. Along with the bones in the box are two books of poetry and a spiral notebook with faded writing and rudimentary camping gear.

X

On a Southwest flight to Kansas City, I am seated across the aisle from a young man. He and I have chosen seats at the back

of the plane. We exchange smiles. He carries no luggage, only a
worn paper sack from which he draws a large, also worn, Ziploc
bag. Visible inside the Ziploc bag are cards and letters and scraps
of paper. I read over his shoulder as he removes various items.
"We've missed you," dated Christmas 1997. I note his name and
address on one of the envelopes: E—— D——, Unit G, ——Hospital. During the course of the flight he sorts through the papers.
The ones he wishes to discard he puts in an airsick bag. On a Palm
Pilot he enters names and addresses and telephone numbers from
the documents.

E. D. has the look of someone who has been away. His
clothes—chinos and a denim shirt—are brand-new. His hair
is newly trimmed and he is pale. He spills a plastic cup of Can-
ada Dry, which splashes me. "I am so very sorry," he says, visibly
upset. "It's okay, really; at least it wasn't coffee." He turns back to
his task. Reading and entering and sorting and saving and dis-
carding. On the back of a postcard of the Painted Desert: "We
will see you soon, E——. Love, Mom and Dad." He turns to me,
"I really like being at the back of the plane. It's safer back here."
I smile in response. When we land at KCI, no one meets him. He
has no baggage at baggage claim. He just walks outside the ter-
minal and disappears into a clear October afternoon. I fight the
desire to follow him, to ask him where he's headed. I have a gig at
the University of Kansas.

The more I glance against strangers the more I am reminded
of Simone Weil's belief that the only question in the universe is:
"What are you going through?"

Dream: September 11, 2002. I am on one of the planes out of Logan, seated next to a flight attendant, who says to me, "I've never missed a day of work, but I guess I won't be going in tomorrow."

An old lady sells bunches of pink and purple sweet peas at a farmers' market in a town on the central coast of California. She comments on my Steinbeck Center shopping bag and tells me she came out here from Arkansas during the dust bowl. All along the route she broadcast the seed for the flowers from the open back of a Ford pick-up. "I reckon I've left my mark," she says.

Sites of Memory

I ask the driver to take me to SFO via the coast highway. Dimity shimmers on the face of the ocean. Incandescence lighting the water. Lines of pelicans glide alongside the bluffs. My usual feelings about leaving are magnified and I am sunk in a deep sadness. Leaving, losing. I lost my island twice in childhood and have always felt out of place, something missing. Someone once said the loss of your country is the greatest loss you can suffer, save the loss of a child. The driver gets me to the airport early. He wishes me safe travel. I smile, thank him. Inside, I find a lounge, make a phone call, drink some Pellegrino, glance through *Der Spiegel*. I check the gate number on the screen and begin the wait for the 9 p.m. Lufthansa flight to Frankfurt.

Seated next to me in business class is a very strange creature. An elderly person—close-cropped white hair, short, round figure, wearing a three-piece scarlet suit, white shirt, and scarlet necktie—who displays studied masculine gestures (jingling change, clearing throat, etc.) but who is almost certainly female. (What male besides Santa, a pimp, or a busker would wear a scarlet suit?) I usually don't give a damn about people's preferences, but my seatmate exudes a strangeness beyond gender matters. We each have a tv with several channels, in English and German. My seatmate is glued to Bugs Bunny in German and laughs loudly, deeply at the wascally wabbit. This irritates me unduly, and I realize soon enough that this person is becoming the target of the misery I feel at having left.

I thumb through a copy of the *International Herald Tribune*. (On this date fifty years ago an American woman jumped from the Eiffel Tower. Ye gods, get a grip, girl!) I order a glass of wine. Flip the channels on the tv. *Dr. No.* Jamaica in 1960 or so. Ursula Andress rising from the waters, knife strapped around her midsection. I see myself back then—in my school uniform, lolling in the volcanic sands. Playing hooky at Cable Hut.

A screen in the front of the cabin announces it is −40° Centigrade in the blackness outside. Occasionally notations of time, temperature, altitude are replaced by the image of a plane and our flight-path, letting us know how far we have come, how far we have left to go. To my right Bugs Bunny, helmeted, blonde-braided, is being Brunhilde. "Ki-ill the wabbit! Ki-ill the wabbit!"—Teutonic Merrie Melody.

APPROACH

There is an extraordinary greenness breaking through cloud cover as we make our approach to Frankfurt. Greenness exists in degrees of vividness, deepness, like the blues of the Caribbean.

One forgets how rural much of Europe still is. We pass over forests, fields, and sight the city in the distance.

On the ground it is a bleak Saturday morning. I am met at the Frankfurt Airport, dark and immense, then driven to campus housing. The university has arranged an apartment in the Gastprofessorenhaus on Wittichweg. The building—like many in these parts built postwar—is a blank, utilitarian space. The apartment likewise. With nothing like a radio or television or cd player. On the desk is the Lufthansa schedule (I feel like Tantalus) and the Everyman edition of *Mansfield Park*. My host returns from the grocery store. I thank him, fighting tears. I collapse into a deep sleep after a good crying jag and wake after three hours or so. I am not someone who minds being alone. In fact, I need it. But this is different. After waking, I take a bath and pour myself a glass of Riesling.

On Sunday the campus is completely deserted. But—*ecco!* I find an Italian restaurant—Campus Pizza—within walking distance of the apartment. It is light, welcoming. What German I knew has deserted me; I found that out on the flight. Here at least I can speak Italian. The restaurant is run by Italians, to the Germans, *auslanders*. Campus Pizza will become my home away from home.

I'm in the middle of Assia Djebar's *So Vast a Prison*. I order a glass of Pinot Grigio, a plate of *vitello tonnato,* and open the book: "Why Pasolini? that is how it was, there is no more to it than that . . . I, an Arab woman, writing classical Arabic poorly, loving and suffering in my mother's dialect, knowing I have to recapture the deep song strangled in the throat of my people, finding it again with images, with the murmur beneath images, I tell myself henceforth, *I am beginning (or I am ending) because in a bed where I was preparing for love, I felt—twenty-four hours later and with the whole Mediterranean Sea between us—the death of Pasolini like a scream, an open-ended scream.*"

The assassination of Pasolini between All Saints' and All Souls'—1975—in a boat basin in Ostia. The "Desperate Vitality" of this poet:

—sono come un gatto bruciato vivo,	I am like a cat burned alive,
pestato dal copertone di un autotreno,	crushed by the tires of a truck, hanged by boys from a fig tree
impiccato da ragazzi a un fico	Death is not
La morte non e	in not being able to
nel non poter comunicare	communicate
ma nel no poter piu essere compresi.	but in no more being able to be understood.

The deep song: *el cante jondo* of Lorca—one with Pasolini—in mode of life, manner of death, depth of song. I love that Djebar speaks across the Mediterranean to the deep song.

No te conoce el toro ni la higuera,	The bull does not know you, nor the fig tree,
ni caballos ni hormigas de su casa	nor the horses, nor the ants in your own house
No te conoce el niño ni la tarde	The boy does not know you, nor the afternoon
porque te has muerte para siempre.	because you have died forever.

(Lorca, "Llanto por Ignacio Sánchez Mejías")

I'd been to Germany only once before. In 1968 when I was twenty-one years old and had recently come through a very serious illness. For the first time I was leaving my parents rather than the other way round, which had been their pattern in my childhood. I could bring those times back, the awful sense of not just being left, but of having absolutely no choice in the matter. Spending hours lying under the mango tree in my mother's mother's front yard, listening, trying to will the sound of their car. The mulatto Scott and Zelda. Since very young I had thought of Europe as my escape route. From that family, its sun-drenched cruelties. My father's palm imprinted across my mouth.

Monday: I visit the American Studies Department. The professor is a big fan of the United States. His office is a study in American iconography, especially southern iconography, especially the Black experience in the American South. Pictures of ribs joints and blues joints. A group picture of German graduate students at Ole Miss, for Faulkner's centenary. Black-and-white photographs of Muddy Waters and Robert Johnson. A pair of boxer shorts made in the design of the American flag. I am observing a pattern (and I don't mean the boxers): A desire among these academics to attempt an internal migration to another country, which country's memory they will define, making themselves at home.

For example: From the course catalogue: Sommersemester 2000: Johannes Gutenberg Universität, Mainz:

> Sites of Memory range from the written page, pictorial representations and photographs, ruins, the human body, to the 2,000 sites of historic significance of the National Historic Landmarks Program or the documents to be preserved under the "Save

America's Treasures Program." . . . As examples we will discuss
— the debate over the Vietnam War Memorial
— the monuments on the Washington Mall as icons of American
civil religion
— Plymouth Rock and the Salem Witch Trials Tercentenary
Memorial: pride and shame (?) in memorizing
— Graceland as a shrine of popular culture. [et al.]

At a reception I am introduced round to a group of English pro-
fessors; one has a comb-over and bad breath and backs me up
against a wall to discuss the Vietnam Memorial in Washington, D.C. I have encountered Professor Sites of Memory. Sites of
Memory is very popular here, now. Invented in the eighteenth
century by German intellectuals, its focus began in South America, then moved north. Alexander von Humboldt was one notable enthusiast. Sites of memory do not include the European landscape, German memory. I am too polite at the moment to ask why
not. Apart from the obvious, this being Germany — Why not the
boat basin in Ostia?

TEACHING

I walk through a miasma of cigarette smoke outside the class-
room. Inside are about fifty students, some with shaven heads and
elaborate tattoos. I feel no affect in the room. My words bounce
back at me. The course is the literature of colonialism: past and
post. I announce the texts: *Heart of Darkness, The Voyage Out,
July's People, No Telephone to Heaven.* I begin: an introduction to
Heart of Darkness, Conrad, Achebe's critique of Conrad, and so
on. My words are met with giggles and whispers. One woman in

the back of the room tries to begin a discussion. She is an older student. Her English makes it difficult for me to understand her ideas. When I ask her to speak up, to speak more slowly, the rest of the class laughs. I talk some more, dismiss them early. I wonder what they expected, who they expected. What do they know of the outside world, word? Walking back to the Gastprofessorenhaus I observe graffiti on a wall outside a dormitory: *SS* etched on the yellow stucco in lightning strokes. The *s* in Deutschland drawn as a swastika. For the six weeks of my residency these will remain on the wall. No one will mention them.

The next day I lecture for an hour and a half on Nation Language, among other things. This is a Caribbean writers course: Walcott, Césaire, Brathwaite. Those three for the most part. I stress the complexity of the work we will be reading. I have found too often that Caribbean writing is assumed to be "easy," when actually it is one of the most complex of literatures. When it *is* literature, that is. As I finish, the class beats a tattoo on their desks. Approval.

THIS JUST IN #1

From the *Frankfurt Allgemeine:*

Asylum Seeker Commits Suicide

An Algerian woman has hanged herself in the transit section of the Frankfurt Airport. . . . The forty year old woman, who was married to an opponent of the current regime in Algeria and had been beaten and raped by the Algerian police, was awaiting political asylum in Germany the past eight months. Her application was turned down because she was unable to recall the date of her first rape.

The campus overlooks the town cemetery. On the map I am given, the cemetery is divided into two sections. Each is colored green. On the larger section there are crosses scattered about. The smaller section bears no such insignia. I take a walk to the smaller section. Inside its gates is a small building, of Moorish design. On its walls, every now and then, is a Star of David and under the star a passage from Psalms. Behind this building are the graves, monuments. This is the *judenfriedhof*. On one monument are the names of the Family Blatt, with their dates, and: *opfer Auschwitz   opfer Riga*   I touch the etched letters, feel the coldness of black stone, see myself in the polished granite. Next to a bench in the center of the *judenfriedhof* someone has left a plastic bag of empty beer cans and other garbage. I pick it up and take it to a trash can.

The smells are of damp earth and lilac and rosemary. Sites of Memory.

ENCOUNTERING A RABBI ON THE STAIRCASE AT THE GASTPROFESSORENHAUS

I had been told by my hosts that there was a rabbi visiting, a guest professor, here each spring to teach Judaic Studies. When he was first appointed, the university did not know where to situate him: the Theology Department was divided into Catholic and Protestant. They put him with the Protestants, this being a Catholic part of Germany—I have been told Mainz is nicknamed "The Rome of the North."

Joke: A man is walking along a dark street in Belfast when he feels the cold steel of a gun barrel at the back of his neck. A voice asks: "Are you Catholic or Protestant?" The man answers: "I'm a Jew." The voice asks: "Are you a Catholic Jew or a Protestant Jew?"

A CONFERENCE ON "TRANSITIONAL IDENTITIES"

The cast of characters includes some Caribbean writers and scholars (both Francophone and Anglophone) and European (for the most part, German) scholars, of literature, as well as ethnography. One chap is a white man who grew up in the Caribbean and now teaches in England. He presents a paper on a work of poetry from the eighteenth century entitled *The Sugar-Cane* by James Grainger, enthusiastic slaveowner. In the paper he argues that Grainger is the literary ancestor of Kamau Brathwaite. Trade winds ruffle the Caribbees. We disagree. The chap turns beet red, trots out his black wife. One participant, an ethnographer from Würzburg, speaks of the need to preserve Caribbean music and suggests that the master tapes be held in Germany for safekeeping in case of revolution. He is serious. The natives grow restless. I cannot resist being trickster: "That seems only fitting given that Bob Marley drove a BMW." Beat. "He said the letters stood for Bob Marley and the Wailers." I gaze the gaze of reverse anthropologist.

My particular problem with the literary participants of the conference is their determination that they read my fiction—and other Caribbean fictions—as autobiography, diluting and undermining the politics of the narrative. They want to reduce the collective to the individual. They want to define who we are: What are "transitional identities" anyway? None of the organizers seems able to respond. Are we seen as lone riders between the rainforest and the Black Forest, the island and the metropole?

I am not a metaphor. My place of origin is not a metaphor. I inhabit my language, my imagination, more and more completely. It becomes me. I do not exist as a text. I am spoken into being—as Léopold Sédar Senghor said of the world. I speak myself into being and with that speech my place of origin. I use this speech to craft fiction, which is not a record of myself, which is self-consciously—self-confidently—political. I do believe in the word, that a new world may be spoken into being.

THE DEPARTMENT SECRETARY

A bosomy, sweet-faced woman invites me to attend the opera with herself and her husband: Wagner's *Flying Dutchman*. She says her husband is Chilean and a scientist and speaks no German and so they communicate in Spanish, in which she is fluent. I ask her where she learned Spanish, and she tells me that after the Second World War the Spanish invited German children to come to Spain to recover from their deprivations. Reward for Guernica? I lie through my teeth and tell her I'm off to Paris. "Pinochet was not so bad," she tells me.

THE BALLAD OF MAUTHAUSEN

On the fifty-fifth anniversary of the liberation of the concentration/death camp Mauthausen in Austria, the Vienna Philharmonic plays Beethoven's Ninth Symphony under the baton of Simon Rattle. The setting for the concert is the quarry at Mauthausen, where Sisyphean exercises were once enacted. At one end of the quarry is a stone staircase of 186 steps. Prisoners were forced to carry rocks up the staircase, often to be pushed backward to their deaths upon reaching the top. The deaths at Mauthausen—estimated at 105,000—Jews, homosexuals, communists, "antisocials"—were of a variety: gas, gunshots, medical experiments, overwork, starvation. Newspapers run editorials: Is the "Ode to Joy" a suitable piece for the memorializing of those thousands?

Has no one heard of *The Ballad of Mauthausen?* Theodorakis's song cycle, words by Iakovos Kambanellis sung by Maria Farandouri, which a lover once gave me. From "Otan Teliossi O Polemos" ("When the War Ends"): "Don't forget me—wait for me, so that we can meet, kiss and walk in the sunny streets among normal, ordinary people . . . when the war ends . . . or when we meet at the gas chamber."

ENCOUNTERING THE RABBI ONCE MORE

He is a very old man. He was a young man in this town in the thirties and with his wife was forced to leave. They ended up in Sonoma. He tells me the university treats him very well. He has been made a senator of the university. He walks with two canes and recently lost his wife of sixty-two years. He is in deep mourning. He tells me that the theology faculty was recently discussing "theodicy": "I simply said to them, 'After the Holocaust you can have no theodicy.'"

MUTTERSTAG

Since I am motherless, I am at loose ends. It's Sunday and I take a walk through the cemetery. In the gentile section are lines of green watering cans, and people are gardening. Weeding, pruning rose bushes, planting. Lilac comes in several shades of purple, as well as white. I find the graves of the burghers, massive, stairs down into vaults. One is a huge pyramid guarded by two sphinxes. Obsidian. Another records a brother fallen at Verdun; another dead in São Paulo forty years later. *Hotel Terminus.*

The Jewish cemetery is a rock garden. Mossed pebbles sit atop monuments. Again I visit, again I am alone but for the resonance of ghosts, stretching back to the seventeenth century.

DINNER IN THE OLD PART OF TOWN

I raise the subject of Günter Grass's recent book *My Century,* which I read in the desert in California to prepare myself for my stay. I am immediately apprised that not much is thought of the book, that it is regarded as a post-Nobel phenomenon. I am told every writer writes a bad book, a self-indulgent expression of greatness, following on the Nobel. I concentrate on my braised rabbit, drink another glass of Kupferberg Gold.

I was particularly struck by Grass's refusal to romanticize the reunification and the adamant notion that I have bumped into here more than once, that the past is past, the domain of but a few thugs.

One of the company invites me to visit the room where Luther once debated Zwingli during the Marburg Colloquy of 1529.

A READING AT THE RATHAUS

The city of Mainz was the site of Gutenberg's invention of moveable type. Thus the name of the university. At the center of the city, near the *rathaus,* a figure dressed in silver lamé robotically mimes Gutenberg, creating a *Metropolis* effect. Mainz is located on the Rhine. Here and there the remnant of Roman walls can be seen. I am reading in the Haifa Room at the *rathaus*—Haifa, I am told, is Mainz's sister city. I am surrounded by murals of old men in long beards, the town seal (in Hebrew) of Haifa. As a gift for my reading, I am given what they tell me is the smallest book in the world: The Lord's Prayer in seven languages. Only about one centimeter square, the book comes with a magnifying glass; its cover is black leather with a gold-embossed cross.

INTERVIEW

I am interviewed by a German woman who has translated my work. She is married to a Rastafarian and tells me she fears for her family; the rage against the *auslander* is palpable. The papers carry stories almost every day. I have a few Turkish and Italian students, children of "guest-workers," who, although born here, are not allowed German citizenship. They tell me of the harassment they experience, the anger they experience. The interviewer tells me she is applying for Jamaican passports for her children to hedge her bets.

THIS JUST IN #2

May 7. A television report from Dachau. Shots of old men wearing yarmulkes marching alongside barracks, spruced up, a sanitized imagery highlighted by May flowers. The past is vivid. A week or so ago there were front-page articles in the paper regarding a ban on pit bulls and other attack dogs. Their owners declared their plans to march through Berlin with the dogs wearing the yellow star — victims, the owners said, of racism. The Jews of Berlin objected; the march was called off. Can there be a collective unconscious?

There will now be guided tours of Room 600 of the Nuremberg District Court on weekends.

Paula Wessely, one of the "most acclaimed" actresses of the twentieth century, has died. Also known as a "voluntary tool" of the Nazis, she possessed a voice known especially for its unique timbre.

BOTANICAL GARDENS

This is a place of astonishing beauty. *Nachtigall,* she of a plain brownness, almost invisible inside her song, trilling within the arms of a flowering chestnut tree. Bullfrogs croak on lily pads. Wild iris. Cobra lilies. Enormous red poppies, with a heart so black it becomes deep purple.

I sit within this beauty and read.

LAST NIGHT

I am taken to a restaurant set in a vineyard which slopes down to the Rhine. We are seated on a glass-enclosed porch. Wine is brought in earthenware jugs, and dark bread and dishes of butter are placed before us. Outside is a plaque to Goethe commemorating his frequenting the place. Across the river is the small town where I lodged with a German family in 1968. I cannot help but feel I am gazing across time at myself. A very young woman who had realized she must someday die.

Outside the windows of the porch there is a sudden storm, black sky, lightning, thunder. The lightning rakes the glass. The valley, lit by lightning, the Rhine, silver. A freight train crosses the valley in the storm. There are children at the table, excited by the train. "Like a child's toy," someone observes. The train, tiny from this distance, chugging along the Rhine. Picturesque as a grove of trees in the American South.

Lynchburg 2003

I. Ota Benga

> There is darkness all around us;
> but if darkness *is*
> and if the darkness is of the forest,
> then the darkness must be good.
>
> —Forest-dweller's song

The poet has a pygmy in her parlor. The poet with the pygmy ("forest-dweller" to you) in her parlor, on her porch, in her celebrated garden where antique roses climb   Crimson Glory   American Beauty   Blaze.   Edged by wild sassafras—one of his gifts to her. Another is wild honey, which he gathers in the woods overlooking the James. What else does he find in those woods? In the forest which is his dwelling place?

I visit this garden in 2003 and find the tailfeather of a mockingbird, beneath a house built for a pair of purple martins.

> **The African Pygmy, "Ota Benga." Age, 23 years. Height, 4 feet 11 inches. Weight, 103 pounds. Brought from the Kasai River, Congo Free State, South Central Africa by Dr. Samuel P. Verner. Exhibited each afternoon during September.**
>
> —*New York Times,* September 10, 1906

The pygmy ("forest-dweller" to you) in the poet's parlor was most recently an inmate at the Bronx Zoo. His company an orang-utan and a gorilla. By night he is caged. Some days he strolls the grounds in a white suit. The children of the city are brought to the zoo; he falls beneath their gaze.

> **There were 40,000 visitors to the park on Sunday. Nearly every man, woman and child of this crowd . . . chased him about the grounds all day, howling, leering, and yelling. Some of them poked him in the ribs, others tripped him up, all laughed at him.**
> —*New York Times,* September 18, 1906

At the bottom of the poet's garden is a pond. A fish pond, where a white-fleshed lotus floats, solid as a stepping stone. A cast-iron head—Ogun's handiwork—decorates one end of the pond. Ecce, Prince Ebo! Gift of W. E. B. DuBois, all the way from Africa. Next to which another African head lay spent—the forest-dweller's homesick own. Flash forward: DuBois passing on the eve of the March—in Ghana—his exile home. Heart heavy.

> **Ota Benga says civilization is all witchcraft . . . asserts New York is not wonderful and that we are all madmen.**
> —*New York World,* September 16, 1906

The poet befriends the forest-dweller. He finds work in a tobacco factory. He teaches the poet's son the skills of living in the out-doors. He teaches children the calls of the wild. He tries to pay a bus driver with a rabbit he pulls from a sack. The driver accepts. By and by—as they used to say in old stories—the African inquires after steamship tickets. He realizes he will never have the money to go home. His is the simplest longing.

On March 20, 1916, at the vernal equinox, he builds a fire in a clearing. He drives the bullet clean through his heart.

Does he use the poet's gun?

OTA BENGA, PYGMY TIRED OF AMERICA
The strange little African finally ended his life at Lynchburg, Va. Once at the Bronx Zoo, his American sponsor found him shrewd and courageous ...
—*New York Times,* July 16, 1916

November 8, 2003. The night of a lunar eclipse. I read the death certificate. The moon blackens. Shot through breast. Name: Otto Bingo! [There was a farmer who had a dog and Bingo was his name—oh. B I N G O And Bingo was his name—oh.]

II. Necropolis

I search the city cemetery; he is nowhere to be found. Not finding him—not wanting to leave "empty-handed?"—I search amid the Confederate dead for the unmarked "Negro Row." A piece of cobalt blue glass—as smooth as beach glass—has worked its way to the surface free of a grave. I pick it up, try to imagine what it once was, decide to leave it behind. I was taught that if you take something from a grave, the departed will follow you home. My boots are caked with red mud.

There was a woman named Jane buried amid the Confederate dead. Slave to a soldier, she is buried alongside other soldiers' slaves.

A black cat jumps from behind a headstone.

"Psst . . . Jane? That you?"

This entire town is a necropolis. Churches and graveyards along-side the Civil War markers—Inner Defenses, Outer Defenses, redoubts and trenches—and just exactly how much blood was shed where Wal-Mart stands. The dead easily outnumber the quick. All eyes are on the afterlife. A place in thrall to death. And the past, far from dead.

III

Over my catfish po'boy at the Jazz Street Grill I overhear from the next table:

WOMAN [who has just visited Monticello]: "Do you know what a fifty-five-year-old woman slave was worth?"

MAN [who has not]: "A dollar fifty?"

WOMAN: "No. Nothing. She couldn't have children and she was slowing down. But some of the plantation owners let the old ones stay on."

MAN: "Oh."

WOMAN [expressing the inevitable; at least *I've* been waiting for it]: "Did you know Thomas Jefferson had children with a slavewoman?"

MAN: "How do they know?"

WOMAN: "They tested their DNA."

MAN: "They had DNA way back then?"

[I start to laugh; the man catches me.]

MAN: "You know why I like this restaurant? Because I like jazz."

IV

On the way back from Roanoke I buy a half gallon of apple cider from an old codger who runs a farmstand. He tells me how to make hard cider. "You wrap the container in newspaper and put it in a cool closet for three months. You'll know it's ready when some gnats—we call them 'drunkards'—start to gather around the jug."

His pick-up is parked next to the farmstand. Bumpersticker: Somewhere in Texas a Village Is Missing Its Idiot.

A Saturday afternoon and a black Chevy Blazer or Ford Explorer pulls out in front of me near Thomas Road Baptist Church. The license plates (vanity, saith the preacher, all is vanity) give the driver away. He waves at his public like a queen of England.

How many people in this town are enthralled, awaiting the Rapture? Will they wake one morning to find themselves all gone?

V. Pools

There were once three public pools in this town: two white, one black. When the word came down to integrate, the burghers of the town decided to fill each pool with dirt and to plant grass. Today, in Riverside Park, across from the remains of the boat—now rusted hulk—that carried Stonewall Jackson's body down the James, a rectangular grave where a swimming pool once was.

And somewhere else in this town an explosion of black-blood-red pooling in a forest clearing.

The Thing behind the Trees

I have been placing this hieroglyph of myself in (different) kinds of settings as an exorcism in an effort to return to the center of life.

— Ana Mendieta, in a letter to a friend

The thing behind the trees was a silhouette, an indentation in the earth where the body of a woman had lain.

I will tell you how I got there.

Some years back, 1998 I think, I was on a book tour, doing readings from a volume of short fiction. I found myself in a bookshop in a small town in western Massachusetts. The audience was small but attentive. The bookshop owner apologized for the size of the group. I replied with my usual "that's okay"—my kind of writing has only in a few instances attracted a crowd—and asked for water.

Ravines. Gullies. Those places you are warned about as a girl. Places where a faceless danger lurks. Early impediment of freedom.

The reading was uneventful. The questions polite. I thanked the bookshop owner, the audience, signed a few books and left. I walked back to the place I was staying, the alumnae house on the campus of a women's college. My editor had attended school there, and I was let in under her auspices. The evening, in January, was frigid and clear. The trees naked of foliage except for the Douglas fir. The alumnae house was chilly, filled with drafts dating back to the late 1800s.

My bed was narrow, the sheets rough, pure white. The desk in the room was stained with dark blue ink. The school literary magazine, *Virginia* (referring to the writer, not the state), had been left on my bedstand, and I fell asleep reading the fiction of very young women.

The next day I took my leave. I stepped outside into the cold of the winter morning and waited for the car service to take me to the airport. The driver was late.

Fifteen, twenty minutes passed, and finally he turned up. In a maroon Chrysler as I recall, a few years old. He was, the publisher had told me, a local man who had his own business carrying passengers to and from the several area airports. He wore a red-and-black-checkered hunting cap and a red-plaid woolen jacket. He spoke nonstop and in the course of things told me about the Burlington factory outlet where he had bought the jacket. He asked me if I wanted to make a detour there. I said no, thank you. He had horn-rimmed spectacles, with black frames. In the midmorning light his teeth glistened. As we drove into the sere landscape, he informed me that we would be taking back roads to the airport. I told him I was afraid I'd miss my flight, that the high-way was much faster than his way, but he refused.

"I know best," he said. "Never had anyone miss a plane yet."

He offered me a drink from his thermos of coffee, but I politely declined. I was feeling uneasy and used politeness to dis-tance myself from him.

We started out on surface roads, passing through small towns, with identical edifices. You know, white-steepled church, one-story brick post office, convenience store, houses with clapboard shingles, brick chimneys, front porches. It must have been early January, for here and there at the curb were the remains of a Christmas tree, dregs of tinsel clinging to the branches, remnants of celebration. In front of the churches, mostly Congregational and Presbyterian, were bulletin boards, announcing the name of the minister, the time of Sunday school and the Sunday service, and the subject of that week's sermon. Each Main Street as reli-able as a stage set.

"Ever been here before?"
"Yes, I have."
"I've lived here all my life. This is good coffee, sure you don't want some?"
"No, thanks."
"My lady friend always sends me off with a thermos of coffee every morning. She's a real beauty. Don't know what I'd do with-out her. My wife of forty years passed a few months ago."

"I'm sorry to hear that. I mean about your wife."

"Yes, good women, the both of them. I was well taken care of. Still am. None of that women's lib stuff for them. You a women's libber?"

"I'm sorry?"

"I don't know who those women think they are."

"I wouldn't know."

"My wife was happy just to be at home. You married? Got kids? I got two. But they're off somewhere."

"No." I wanted to say in answer to the "Got kids?"—"None that I'm aware of"—but didn't want to risk the joke.

"Well, when you get married, when you have kids, I don't think you'll want to be on the road. What were you doing at that college anyway?"

"Seeing friends." I lied—again.

Women mourn, men replace. Where had I heard that aphorism?

"The people who hired me said you're a writer?"

"Yes, I am."

"What kind of things do you write?"

"All kinds."

"You write about murders?"

"I have done."

"Then we'll take a detour. You don't want to miss this."

"Look, I really need to make that flight. I have got to be in New York by early afternoon. I really don't have time to take any detour."

"What? You seeing your boyfriend?"

"I have an appointment I can't afford to miss." I had a book signing at Three Lives, in the Village.

"Believe me, you'll thank me for the detour. I told you, I never had a passenger miss their plane."

There was silence. I did not know what to say.

Then: "This happened last April. They never did find out who did it."

Of course. I was still, silent. I knew what was coming. Something mundane, horrific.

"Women should never take dirt roads."

He paused, looked at me in the rearview mirror. "Didn't you hear me?"

I nodded, said nothing.

Somewhere outside Holyoke he turned onto a back road. Bare birches lined each side of it. Sunlight glinted across the road, here and there lighting bits of gravel.

The heat in the car was getting to me. I cracked the window, breathed deeply the wintry air. Hoping I could wake up from this, find myself back in my virginal quarters.

"She was taking a walk. It happened in the spring, April. I guess I already said that." As he spoke, he continued to gaze at me in the mirror.

"I don't have to tell you what happened. Out in the night, alone, walking on a dirt road. What was she thinking?"

I finally spoke. "How did they know she was alone?"

"Oh, they knew all right. They knew."

He drove about a mile and then pulled over into a shallow ditch.

"Why are you stopping?"

"Get out; you need to see this."

"I really don't need to."

"Look, I went out of my way to show you."

"I need to catch that flight."

"You need to see this first."

The airport—it seemed a timebend away.

He stood outside the window glaring at me. I dug my nails into the palms of my hands, inducing stigmata.

Dark places. Woods. Forest. Deserted places. Beaches. Dunes. Well-lit places. Interruption of solitude.

Making love with another woman in a clearing in the woods. Through the trees the velvet pelt of a doe. I say nothing. I try to ignore the fear of being happened upon by hunters but cannot. My passion is quelled. "Is there something wrong?" she asks.

"It's right behind these birches. You can still see her shape in the ground. Ground's frozen from an early frost. Looks like the place a deer was sleeping."

He opened the door and beckoned me out.

Is she here? Does the frozen earth vibrate with her?

Am I to play accommodating female—placate him—hope no ill befalls me?

Suddenly I feel a kinship with this woman. Not sister-hood, more like fellow traveler. This is where the power lies. I try to bring her into the foreground of my mind, driving him backward.

I get out of the car.

"Who was she?"

"Local woman. Bookkeeper or something. About forty or so."

"Who found her?"

"Couple of kids taking a shortcut through the woods. She was a mess. All maggoty and bloated." He shook his head.

He led me into the woods and there it was: the thing behind the trees. Naked. The silhouette of a woman frozen into the landscape. Nearby the frozen tunnel-rise of a burrowing animal. Piles of iced twigs and leaves. Nest of burned-out cigarettes.

"Don't tell me," I say, averting my eyes from her outline. "They were freckle-faced, wore striped T-shirts, carried superhero lunchboxes . . . cliché."

"Don't know. What's a cliché?"

"Something tired. Very tired."

"Okay."

Heat the opposite of Cold.

A woman artist ventures into the woods, an open field, a deserted hillside, outlining her body—her body into the terrain, creating another silhouette. Lighting the outline. Exploding the contours of her breasts, belly, vulva—those that make her female—with gunpowder. Darkening earth. Her self a blasting cap.

Flaming silhouette, white flowers along the lines of her body, floating on a raft downriver.

Silhouette of Ashes, scorched, return to earth, release of soul through fire. Exploding *anima*.

Finally: Her imprint on a New York City sidewalk behind two ancient ginkgoes. Her husband said she fell while drunk. Some question his version.

Back in the woods I play it safe. I tell the driver thank-you and am ashamed, but caution overrules any questions I might have: Does he know more than he is saying? Does he bring others to this site? Did he know her? The viewing over, we walk back to the road.

The end is uneventful. We get back into the car and continue to the airport in blessed silence.

In My Heart, a Darkness

I

The most important interracial relationship I have is within myself. I move through the landscape a double agent, where I listen and learn.

On a plane on the way to Houston, I overhear a conversation between two men. Actually, it's more of a monologue. The speaker is American, holding forth to a European about Texas history: Sam Houston, Santa Ana, and the Battle of San Jacinto.

Houston's troops—he says—killed "six hundred goddamn Mexicans." The Texans were able to accomplish this because the Mexicans were taking a siesta (caught napping), and Santa Ana was "fucking this little mulatto gal from one of the plantations."

The "little mulatto gal became known as the yellow rose of Texas."

This little mulatto gal adds that bit of lore to her store of a million items. In the words of Bessie Head (another little mulatto gal): I am the "collector of such treasures."

From *The Hornes:*

Lena began the civil rights decade with a well-aimed missile to a bigot's head—*not* a nonviolent protest. . . . Lena overheard a waiter telling a boorish drunk that he would be with him in a minute, as soon as he'd finished "serving Lena Horne." But the drunk wanted instant service. "Where is Lena Horne, anyway?" the drunk wanted to know. "She's just another nigger," he added. At that point Lena stood up and said, "Here I am, you bastard! Here's the nigger you couldn't see," and proceeded to hurl a large glass ashtray at the man's head.[1]

You go, girl.

Glenn Ligon: at the Carnegie Museum of Art: **We are the ink that gives the white page a meaning.** Repeated and repeated as the letters darken the white canvas. Do whites rely on blacks for a sense of being. Why does the black image exist in the white mind.

Across town at the Warhol: **Without Sanctuary.** A pictorial reliquary. Repetitiveness of images: rope, elongated bodies, bowed heads. Still bodies against excited spectators. The only movement the activity of the mob. The effect is numbing. What of the struggle before. The pleas for mercy. The dragging through the dirt. Last words: pleas, fury. But these are the stuff of souvenir — what wants to be remembered. Stillness, silence is essential not to rattle the white imagination.

With very few exceptions I have not failed to be disappointed in my relationships with white people — American and European. Very few of my best friends are white. I learned at an early age to protect myself. I have learned over the years that most white

---

1. Gail Lumet Buckley, *The Hornes* (New York: Knopf, 1986), 242.

people have internalized supremacist values, take their skin privilege for granted. That many of the well-meaning among them fall into the Schweitzerian category: Albert Schweitzer remarking that yes, the African was his brother, albeit his younger brother. The elder European brother striding through his medical colony, while strains of Bach fall on native ears. Humanitarian, perhaps, but with a smidge of Kurtz.

Others express their solidarity diffidently: In Kentucky once at a women writers' conference I attended a reading by Sonia Sanchez. As she read her prose poem "Norma,"[2] about the destruction of brilliance in a young black woman, I found myself weeping, out of control. Later, a white woman approached me and said she had seen my response to the poem and wanted to come over and comfort me but "I was afraid you'd kill me."

I gave the keynote at a conference several years ago; the focus of the conference was the writing of the white American antiracist Lillian Smith, a volume of whose work I had edited in the late 1970s. On the final day, at the final panel, a dapper little white southern gentleman who had known Miss Lillian and had witnessed her efforts to bring the races together in her home in northern Georgia raised his hand and inquired, why was the use of the word *nigger* off-limits for whites? My goodness, in Miss Lillian's own living room he had heard Eslanda Robeson refer to her husband as "My Nigger Paul" (he repeated this three times)—if

---

2. Sonia Sanchez, "Norma," in *homegirls and handgrenades* (New York: Thunder's Mouth Press, 1984), 19ff.

she could do that, then what was wrong with this dapper little man doing likewise? I waited for the chair of the panel, a white woman, to speak, but she appeared frozen and so I presumed to address the question. I asked the little man if he did not understand the difference between Eslanda Robeson's use of the word and his own desire. I pressed: Why did he want the privilege of utterance? The chair defrosted, addressing the little man: "I think what Michelle is trying to say . . ."

Sometimes it's best to keep one's distance, play the fool, the trickster, Anansi, the crafty spider—the Signifying Monkey—

II

TEN SIMPLE TESTS
(EARLY DETECTION MAY SAVE YOUR ASS)

1. You repeat the African-American legend that Ava Gardner was a Black woman passing for white.

The recipient of this news may react with disbelief.

What about Linda Darnell? Dorothy Lamour? Joseph Cotton?

You abandon African-American legend and dig in: Cary Grant? Marlon Brando? Marilyn Monroe? Ingrid Bergman?

You wait for: What are you talking about? Are you crazy? Nuts? Fucking with me?

Why on earth should it matter?

2. You are asked at a dinner party about your background.

You respond that your great + 5 grandfather on your father's side was the youngest son of a British earl, and since he could not inherit the family estate, he emigrated to Jamaica to seek his fortune.

"Ahhhh . . ."

You continue that the ancestors on your mother's side hailed from Africa.

"Ohhhh . . ."

3. Allow how you once went through a village north of Boston and poured buckets of white paint over the lawn jockeys in front of the country club in the dead of night.

Whitefacing private property. "Weren't you afraid you'd get caught?" Don't they realize the irresistibility, the necessity of such an act?

Does anyone raise the historicity of the lawn jockey: shining a light for General Washington?

While we're on the subject of defacing, ask the gathered company how many realized that the Blacks in *Birth of a Nation* were played by white actors in blackface?

Note their reaction to the news.

What do they think about Bert Williams applying burnt cork to his face?

4. Invent a board game: The search for Michael Jackson's nose. Roll the dice and advance your counter from Gary, Indiana, and a little round-faced black boy, to Neverland, California, and a Peter Pan incarnadine (a word, according to Webster's, that means

"pink, flesh-colored"). Are the other players able to see the (black) humor embedded in the self-hatred? Or is the man with the plasticine face only pitied?

5. Discuss Toni Morrison. Tell them that when you read *The Bluest Eye* you want to put your hand into the book and draw out Pecola Breedlove and hold her and rock her and tell her you will make everything right for her. And then you weep because it is too late. And you have the blues.

The [Blues]t Eye

[Blues]tone road   [Bluest] one   Belovéd   Be loved.

When Morrison is awarded the Nobel Prize, what's the buzz at a New York cocktail party?

6. Image from 1985: Old man in Philadelphia on the 6 o'clock news, his 500-disc jazz collection melted by a percussion grenade employed to destroy MOVE. Does the assembled company know about MOVE? About John Africa? What do they think about it? Have they read the work of John Edgar Wideman? "Oh, yes, *Brothers and Keepers*. The one about his brother in prison for murder." Right.

7. Mention at a conference that Heathcliff was a Black man and gauge the response. Remind the audience of the signals Emily Brontë sends. Suggest the source of Heathcliff's fury—not romantic rejection but the trading in human souls (his people) during his three-year absence from Wuthering Heights. Bring it home with the fact that the actual house in which the novel is

based was the homestead of a slave trader. Why does Mr. Earn-shaw travel to Liverpool to attend to business? Why not Brad-ford, Leeds?

Remind them further—while we're on the Brontës—that the madwoman in the attic was actually the mad Blackwoman in the attic. Confined. Furious.

8. Compare O. J. Simpson, Wilt Chamberlain, Robert Mapple-thorpe's headless "Man in Polyester Suit." Recite the text from Glenn Ligon's 1993 *Mudbone (Liar):*

> Niggers had the biggest dicks in the world, and they were try-ing to find a place where they could have they contest. And they wasn't no freak, they didn't want everybody looking. So they walked around looking for a secret place. So they walked across the Golden Gate Bridge and the nigger seen that water and made him wanna piss. One said, "Man, I got to take a leak." And he pulled his thing out and was pissing. Other nigger pulled his out, took a piss.
> One nigger said, "Goddamn, this water cold!"
> The other nigger say, "Yeah, and it's deep too!"[3]

Do they weep for Emmett Till in his watery grave? Can they connect the absurd with the horror?

Do they understand what Dany Laferrière means when he says: "You're not born black, you get that way"?[4]

---

3. In *Black Male: Representations of Masculinity in Contemporary American Art,* edited by Thelma Golden (New York: Whitney Museum of American Art, 1994), 57.

4. Dany Laferrière, *How to Make Love to a Negro* (Toronto: Coach House Press, 1987), 117.

9. The Venus Hottentot. Dorothy Dandridge. Billie Holiday. What elements of connection can the assembled company name between these three? How is Josephine Baker related to these three? How does she diverge? Is it racist to refer to La Bakaire as the Signifying Monkey? What do you think of her "Rainbow Tribe"?

10. What was the Red Summer of 1919? When and why did Frederick Douglass and Sojourner Truth have the following exchange:

s: Frederick! Is God dead?
f: No, God is not dead and therefore slavery must end in blood.

What do they think of John Brown? Remind them of Lorraine Hansberry's longing that the American liberal become the American radical. What's the holdup?

III

So much for lightheartedness. Trickery. The Signifying Monkey signs off.

For me friendship is the most precious bond between two individuals. The basis of this bond is trust. Nothing can destroy the trust I place in another human being more than my realization that the racism he or she has imbibed through his or her place in society as a white citizen is very much alive and well; with this, trust is irrevocably breached. This has happened in my life too many times to recount, and so I approach friendship with a white person with more than a dash of cynicism. But my situation is a peculiar one. As a light-skinned un-American—Afro-Saxon—I have been accused of wanting to be black. I have been told time and again that I don't look like a real Jamaican, nor do I speak like one, nor are my cultural references located solely in the Caribbean. All that means is that the template cut by the white imagination—European or American—cannot accommodate my appearance, speech patterns, or intellect as a West Indian. And when the white imagination is disrupted by matters of race, it becomes agitated. Its sense of neatness is disturbed. When the Other appears to be the One. Apocalypso.

Like Derek Walcott's "fortunate traveller," I may become homeless. To that I would reply that the sea is my home, as are the volcanoes that create the islands, erupting from the sea.

IV

Intimacy suffers. I have practiced my own version of safe sex. Protecting myself with language, wit. This lends a certain lack of spontaneity to a private life, but at least I don't hear remarks about the "neat" positions I can achieve beneath the limbo pole. The system, needless to say, is not foolproof.

V

The theme of interraciality—of heritage and relationship—runs throughout my work. In my novels, the forging of friendship across lines of race and class—Clare and Zoe in *Abeng;* Clare and Harry/ Harriet in *No Telephone to Heaven;* Mary Ellen Pleasant and John Brown in *Free Enterprise*—comprise political acts.

In the latter two novels these friendships, hard-won—between a light-skinned woman and a Black man, and an African-American woman and a white American man—move from the privacy of relationship into public acts of insurrection. Each individual motivated by the agape celebrated by Che Guevara.

I see these friendships as existing on a continuum: culminating in the truly revolutionary connection between Mary Ellen Pleasant and John Brown. Their love for each other—which is based in history—is an act of revolution. When they put this love into action, it informs their revolutionary mission—nothing more nor less than the overthrow of the slaveholding states and the release from bondage of the many thousands.

"In the end we were two people with love for each other. It was that simple. That much of a wonder. And while I did not agree with J. B.'s vision of the dark-skinned future, I never for a minute distrusted his love.

"I have grown so weary of interrupted conversations. That is what death is. It breaks off words between people. It leaves you with a longing for one last talk, or two, or three. A chance to say, 'I do love you. I always will.'

"I was down South when I heard they had hanged him. I spent the day, head down, left foot dragging, immersed in memory. Can you hear me? I said aloud.

"⸱ n he was captured there was a piece of paper in his ⸱h my words on it. 'The axe is laid at the foot of the ⸱e first blow is struck, there will be more money

⸱ a farewell, but at least a promise."[5]

⸱rise (San Francisco: City Lights Books, 2004),

Questions must be asked: Why is this friendship a historical secret. Why has John Brown been pictured a madman, scoundrel, or worse. Why is Mary Ellen Pleasant disappeared.

I assure the reader I did not make this friendship up. When I visited Mary Ellen Pleasant's grave in Napa and saw her epitaph—chosen by her—it rocked me for the exceptional possibilities it represented, and I quoted it twice in *Free Enterprise;* once at the very end:

> she . . . would one day abide in Napa, overwhelmed by a white oleander, arched by the thorns and fruit of a wild blackberry bush, each growing from her. The berries in season staining the white marble of her gravestone, the black juice running into the letters she chose,
>
> SHE WAS A FRIEND OF JOHN BROWN[6]

No more, no less. Such friendship is a triumph of imagination—on every level an act of liberation.

---

6. Ibid., 213.

Born in Kingston, Jamaica, **Michelle Cliff** has lectured at many universities and was Allan K. Smith Professor of English Language and Literature at Trinity College in Hartford. She is the author of the acclaimed novels *Abeng, No Telephone to Heaven,* and *Free Enterprise,* as well as two collections of short fiction, *Bodies of Water* and *The Store of a Million Items.* She lives in California.